"BECOMING BEST FRIENDS WITH YOUR IGUANA, SNAKE, OR TURTLE"

BY BILL GUTMAN

ILLUSTRATED BY
ANNE CANEVARI GREEN

Pet Friends
The Millbrook Press
Brookfield, Connecticut

The author would like to thank Bob Bowker and Larry Wieder for sharing both their knowledge and long-standing experience in handling and living with iguanas and reptiles. Their help in producing an accurate and informative text was immeasurable.

Library of Congress Cataloging-in-Publication Data

Gutman, Bill.
Becoming best friends with your iguana, snake, or turtle / by Bill Gutman.
p. cm. – (Pet friends)
Includes bibliographical references (p.).
ISBN 0-7613-1862-3 (lib. bdg.)
1. Iguanas as pets—Juvenile literature. 2. Snakes as pets—Juvenile literature.
2. Turtles as pets—Juvenile literature. [1. Iguanas as pets. 2. Snakes as pets.
3. Turtles as pets. 4. Pets.] I. Title.
SF459.I38 G88 2001
639.3'9—dc21
00-061298

Published by The Millbrook Press, Inc.
2 Old New Milford Road
Brookfield, Connecticut 06804
www.millbrookpress.com

UNDERSTANDING YOUR PETS

Animals have always played a major role in people's lives. In earlier days, animals did a great deal of work. Oxen pulled the plows that tilled the fields. Horses provided transportation. Dogs were used to guard people and herds of cattle or flocks of sheep. Wherever there were humans, there were usually animals, too.

Today, animals are still a big part of many people's lives. Some still work. Others are kept in zoos or on game farms. And countless millions of animals are simply family pets.

There is much more to pet care than a simple feeding and housing. Whether you have a dog, a cat, a bird, tropical fish, a hamster, a gerbil, a guinea pig, or even a horse or pony, you owe it to that animal to learn all you can about it. Obviously animals can't tell you their feelings. You have to guess what they are thinking and feeling by the way they are acting—by their sounds, their movements, and by changes in their behavior.

This is very important if you want to have a happy, healthy pet that will live out its natural life span. The *Pet Friends* series will not only discuss basic animal care, it will also strive to show what your pet thinks and feels as it lives its life with you.

YOUR PET IGUANA, SNAKE, AND TURTLE

Iguanas, snakes, and turtles have become very popular pets. They are, however, quite different from dogs, cats, birds, hamsters, and most other animals kept in homes. Iguanas, snakes, and turtles are reptiles. They belong to a classification of animals that are cold-blooded. Unlike mammals (cats, dogs, humans), reptiles cannot expend energy to keep their own bodies at a stable temperature. Instead, they must absorb heat from the environment in order to warm their bodies to the optimum temperatures that will assure their good health.

Because of this and other special needs, reptiles are not the easiest pets to keep and care for. In the wild, these animals have survived for millions of years leading relatively simple lives. In their own environment, they spend their time searching for food, regulating their body temperatures, avoiding their natural enemies, and reproducing. Unlike some other animals, living in captivity isn't always easier for reptiles. Unless they are cared for properly, they will slowly weaken and die.

Some people have a natural fear of reptiles. Iguanas can look fierce, and some relatives of the iguana are, indeed, dangerous. Snakes frighten some people by their very appearance—the way they slither through the grass, always flicking their tongues in and out. In addition, there are some snakes whose bite carries a

deadly poison. Turtles are often perceived as slow moving, dim-witted animals that don't do much more than sit around.

Yet these animals became popular pets during the 1980s and 1990s. A recent survey estimates that some 7.3 million pet reptiles are owned by about 3 percent of all households in the United States. People buy reptiles for a variety of reasons. If you love animals, you can certainly be fascinated by these ancient creatures and the way they live and survive. However, you certainly can't look upon them the same way you would a dog, cat, or bird. Reptiles are different.

To fully enjoy a reptile as a pet, you must know a great deal about it. Because reptiles have not lived alongside man for hundreds of years—as have dogs and cats—they are not domesticated animals. That means you must create an environment for them that closely resembles their environment in the wild. It takes real knowledge of the animal to do this properly. You must know how to allow it to maintain its body temperature, how to feed it, and how to house it. Many people who own reptiles don't know these things. They make mistakes and the animal suffers.

Whether you have an iguana, a snake, or a turtle, that animal must depend on you for its survival. Reptiles aren't easy pets, but they can be fascinating animals that you can proudly show to your friends. However, it's important that you learn all you can about them so that the animal will be healthy and happy. That, in turn, will make you happy.

THE DANGER OF SALMONELLA

Salmonella is the name given to a genus of infectious bacteria, first isolated in 1885. There are several species, the most common of which causes salmonella gastroenteritis. This is a type of food poisoning that can cause abdominal pain, fever, nausea, vomiting, and diarrhea. The incubation period (the time it takes to show symptoms) is 8 to 48 hours, with an attack lasting from three to seven days. Mild cases can be treated with medication to stop diarrhea. More severe cases can require antibiotics.

In most cases, salmonella is transmitted through contaminated foods, such as poultry and eggs. Careful cleaning and thorough cooking of food will prevent salmonella infections. There is, however, another source of salmonella that many people don't know. A high proportion of reptiles are carriers of salmonella. Anyone who has a reptile as a pet (including iguanas, snakes, and turtles) must take certain precautions to avoid the possibility of contamination.

There is no guarantee that any reptile is free of salmonella. This includes imported as well as domestically bred animals. If you have a reptile as a pet, you must assume that it is a potential carrier of salmonella bacteria. It is suggested that certain categories of people avoid *all* contact, direct or indirect, with any reptile. These categories include the following:

- Infants and children up to 5 years of age. Some experts say up to 8 years.
- Anyone with HIV/AIDS or other immune system disorders.
- Women who are pregnant because of the risk to the fetus.
- Elderly, frail, or people with poor nutrition.
- People who are receiving or who have recently received antibiotic treatment.

As with many other bacterial infections, the very young and very old are the most susceptible. Thus very young children should not have a reptile as *their* pet. They should also not be allowed to handle the animal if it belongs to an older brother or sister. However, some precautions can be taken to avoid possible salmonella contamination. The rules are fairly simple to learn, but they must be followed every day and without fail. Here are some basic tips to avoid salmonella contamination when you have a reptile as a pet:

- Always wash your hands with disinfectant soap and hot water after handling your reptile.
- Wash for at least 30 seconds and use an antibacterial soap whenever possible.
- Never wash with just water only.
  Keep reptiles out of the kitchen and away from surfaces where human food is stored, prepared, or served.
- Do not use the kitchen sink to clean reptile accessories or cage materials.
- Keep reptile enclosures, water and food bowls, as clean as possible.
- If you have any open cuts or sores on your hands, use rubber gloves when handling your reptile or its accessories.
- When washing reptiles' cages and accessories, avoid-splashing water on your face.
- Do not use bathtubs or shower stalls for reptile-related chores unless you thoroughly disinfect it afterward.

Do you get the idea? The possibility of salmonella infection is something you must always be aware of when you own a reptile of any kind. You and your family should know what precautions to take and make them part of your everyday routine when handling your pet.

IGUANAS

Iguana is the common name for the larger lizards of the iguana family. The most popular iguana kept as a pet is, by far, the green iguana. It is found mainly in Central and South America, living in the tropical rain forest. These ancient animals can grow as large as 6 feet (1.8 meters), from head to tail, and have compressed bodies with a row of leathery spines from the neck to the tail. They have distinct eyelids, large external eardrums, and conspicuous throat pouches, or dewlaps. Each leg has five toes with sharp claws.

A young iguana has a bright green color. This helps hide them among the bright green leaves of the rain forest. They are also capable of quick movements and have excellent eyesight. These traits help them avoid capture by predators.

As the iguana gets older and matures, its color becomes a more muted green. Mature iguanas are known for their impressive courting and defensive displays. They raise their bodies and bob their heads vigorously. The tail of the mature iguana is long and powerful.

Young iguanas stay near the ground, blending in with the green leaves. More mature specimens prefer a higher, less dense habitat, moving into the trees, usually near water. The species is diurnal, active during daylight hours. They spend their time

basking in the sun, finding food, and avoiding predators. In some areas, the predators are human beings, who value both the flesh and the eggs as food.

Green iguanas are largely vegetarians, finding an abundance of plant matter to eat in the lush rain forest. In the wild, however, they will occasionally eat insects and small rodents. To keep these iguanas as pets, you must take care to create an environment that is as close to the rain forest as possible.

CHOOSING AN IGUANA AS A PET

Green iguanas have been popular pets since the early 1980s. The problem is that people don't always get them for the right reasons. When you go to a pet shop to buy an iguana, you will usually find yourself looking at baby iguanas, maybe just two months old, and only 5 to 6 inches (13 to 15 cm) long. For this reason, many people think they will be an easy pet for a youngster to care for.

Bob Bowker, a naturalist with a lifetime of experience keeping and handling reptiles, thinks there is another reason people choose these animals as pets.

"Reptiles generate a kind of fascination for people because they are different," Bowker says. "In that sense, they give the owner a sense of being different. They have something completely unlike the usual dog, cat, or hamster. In addition, people are often told at pet shops that iguanas are pets that require little attention. Nothing could be further from the truth."

Before deciding on an iguana for a pet, you should know what the animal is like and how you must care for it. In picking the animal you want, there are also characteristics you should look for. It's best for a first-time owner to begin with a young iguana.

According to Bob Bowker, you should handle the iguanas for sale and pick one that is reasonably calm. "If you have an extremely nervous animal, chances are it won't tame down," he said. "I also suggest you try to get a female. When males become sexually mature, they tend to bite more so than females. When they are breeding, the males bite the females behind the neck simply to hold on to them. If they hold on to you in a similar way, they can give you a bad bite."

At the same time, Bowker says, iguanas take to handling well, better than other species of lizards. "Some of them bond closely with their owners and, if given up, will stop eating and literally die of a broken heart."

There are still other things to do when choosing an iguana. You should touch and move the animal's limbs. They should feel as if they have good muscle tone. If they feel almost brittle, like twigs, the animal may already be ill. The eyes should be clear,

and there should be no swellings on the body. A swelling can indicate a calcium deficiency, which can be a serious condition for an iguana. The inside of the mouth should be bright pink with no sign of infection.

If you find a healthy iguana and take it home, your job is just beginning.

HOME SWEET HOME

Setting up the right home for your iguana takes time and some real knowledge about the animal's natural habitat. People still feel you can stick a baby iguana in a 10-gallon (38-liter) aquarium, put in a "hot rock," a tree branch, a cup of water, and you're all set. Unfortunately, it doesn't work this way. What people don't realize is that their baby iguana is going to grow quickly and can live for up to 15 years. Therefore, what may be a good home today will be too small a year from now. To house an iguana properly, you must often change its environment as it grows.

"The enclosure must be large enough for the iguana to go from a basking area to a cool-down area away from the sun or light source," Bob Bowker explains. "In the wild, they go from sun to shade, sometimes every ten minutes. It's an instinct, and they will do this for most of the day. There should also be a large vessel of water. Since most homes are too dry for tropical animals, iguanas also enjoy being misted with warm water once or twice a day."

If you plan to use a glass aquarium, do not start with a 10- or 20-gallon (38- or 76-liter) size. The iguana will outgrow this size in a few months. You will need at least a 60-gallon (27-liter) aquarium or a 40- or 50-gallon (151- or 189-liter) terrarium. If you build a custom enclosure, it should have at least three solid

I **HEARD** THEY WERE LOOKING FOR A BIGGER HOUSE...

sides. Most experts agree that this first enclosure will only be good for a year. Then you will need something larger. Even a 100-gallon (379-liter) aquarium will only be satisfactory for about 18 months. So the green iguana is not a pet that can be kept in the corner of your room for years.

The older iguanas get, the higher up they like to be. You can add branches of various sizes, but they should be disinfected before they are added to the enclosure. You can do this by soaking the branches in bleach for 24 hours, then in clean fresh water for another day. After they dry in a warm room for two or three days, they will be ready.

Some people will also build shelves at various heights in the enclosure so that the iguana can climb up and sit on them. Young iguanas also like a hiding spot, a place where they can go to be safely out of view. Hiding logs can be purchased at a pet shop, or a simple, empty cardboard box can be used. These too will have to be replaced as the iguana grows.

You must also be careful with what you put on the bottom of the enclosure. Some people will introduce wood or bark chips, which are used with many small animals. For an iguana, however, this won't work. There is a chance the iguana will ingest some of the chips, as it tends to lick things when exploring its surroundings. Chips or bark can become stuck in the gut, making it impossible for the iguana to digest food. This can lead to a life-threatening situation.

It's best to use something that is easily disinfected and inexpensive to replace. Many experts recommend Astroturf, the artificial grass carpet used in many sports stadiums. With Astroturf, you can have several pieces cut to size and rotate them. That way, while you are cleaning and disinfecting one piece, you can replace it immediately with the other.

The basic enclosure is only one piece to the puzzle. A number of other factors are just as important to maintain a happy and healthy iguana.

HOW DO I PROVIDE HEAT AND LIGHT FOR MY IGUANA?

Because reptiles are cold-blooded animals, having a proper heat source in place is extremely important. In the wild, the iguana gets both the heat and light it needs from the sun. The heat from the sun is necessary for the iguana to regulate its body temperature, which it generally keeps in the 90 degree F (32°C) range, but never over 100 degrees F (38°C). The heat from the sun also activates bacteria in the iguana's hind gut. These bacteria begin to consume the fibrous vegetable matter and help the iguana digest its previously eaten meal.

Like many other reptiles, iguanas are unable to process dietary calcium for use in their bones. Iguanas need to absorb the ultraviolet (UV) radiation from the sun to produce vitamin D_3. This enables them to absorb calcium from the intestinal tract. Without the UV radiation, the iguana will only be able to assimilate a small portion of calcium, no matter how much is

consumed in the diet. Once it begins to become calcium deficient, its system begins to "uptake" calcium from the bones. This eventually will lead to metabolic bone disease, which can cripple and eventually kill the iguana.

How, then, do you assure that your pet is getting the proper amount of heat and the correct kind of light? Of course, if you live in a warm-weather climate or a place where the summers are warm, you can put the iguana's enclosure outside. That way, your pet can sun itself as it would in nature. If you do this, however, you must be careful.

"The sun can kill an iguana in 30 minutes or less if its internal temperature rises above 100 degrees," Bob Bowker explains. "If your animal is outside, you must not only have a completely screened-in enclosure, but a large shaded area for it to escape the sun. Then the iguana can go in and out of the sun, heating and cooling, much as it would do in the wild."

If you cannot put your animal outside, then you must use artificial means to enable it to raise its body temperature. One thing you should definitely *not* use is the hot rock. This is a synthetic rock that is heated electrically and sold in most pet shops. It is often recommended for reptiles. Hot rocks, however, do not heat the animal properly and can actually burn it. Basking animals like iguanas need a heat source from above. For this purpose, hot rocks are useless.

A normal incandescent lightbulb can serve to heat the enclosure if it is placed correctly. In most cases, a bulb in the 75–150 watt range will suffice. It should be placed in "worklight" reflector hoods that can clamp right onto the enclosure. Again, you must be careful not to overdo it. For example, a 250-watt infrared heating bulb placed 10 inches (25 cm) from the basking spot can literally cook the iguana.

To monitor the heat, you can place small reptile thermometers within the enclosure. One should be placed directly in the basking spot to make sure the temperature never goes over 100 degrees. If your room is warm in the summer, you may have to use a smaller lightbulb. If you see your iguana panting, it is too hot. Panting is not normal behavior for the iguana.

Never think that because your room is warm for you (70–72 degrees F, or 21–22°C) it is sufficient for your iguana. At this temperature, its gut will putrefy and the iguana eventually will die. Ceramic heating elements, heating pads set to low and with a towel over them, as well as space heaters are other ways to keep the iguana's environment warm enough.

The proper light is also very important for an iguana to remain healthy. The sun, of course, provides the ultraviolet radiation the animal needs. This, however, is not always possible. Window glass and plastic barriers filter out most of the UV radiation from natural sunlight. If your animal is outside with just a wire or mesh top on its enclosure, then the sun is perfect. Otherwise, you must provide the correct light by artificial means.

Artificial ultraviolet lights must be fluorescent bulbs. Several companies now make special ultraviolet lamps for reptiles. These should be placed 8–12 inches (20–30 cm) away from your iguana wherever it spends the most time. Never place the lamp more than 18 inches (46 cm) from the animal. If you have a free-roaming iguana, or one in a very large enclosure, ask an expert for tips on placing the UV lights. Remember, the UV light is absolutely necessary for the animal to absorb the proper amount of dietary calcium from its digestive tract. Without it, you will have a sick animal, sooner or later.

WHAT CAN I FEED
MY IGUANA?

As with other animals that have not been kept as pets for a long time, there is some debate on the best way to feed an iguana. The biggest mistake many people make is feeding a diet of lettuce, especially iceberg lettuce. If you begin giving an iguana lettuce, it will eat it to the exclusion of everything else. That results in poor nutrition.

Iguanas will eat a mainly vegetarian diet. Various combinations of greens and root vegetables are usually recommended. One basic iguana "salad" consists of one part shredded parsnip, one part shredded green beans or peas, one part shredded squash (butternut is recommended), one part alfalfa pellets (sold as rabbit food), and one-half part shredded fruit (figs are recommended). This type of mixture will provide the iguana with enough protein and is nutritionally balanced. It should still be supplemented with a pinch of calcium carbonate and reptile vitamins.

In addition, you can mix some greens into the basic salad. They can be dandelion greens, watercress, escarole, mustard greens, or collard greens. Mix these up so that the animal is not eating the same thing every day. Others recommend root vegetables such as carrots, turnips, rutabagas, beets, beans, and sweet potatoes as a basic mixture to be fed with a variety of greens.

There is also another way to feed today. "There are both pelleted and powdered commercial iguana diets that require no additional supplements," Bob Bowker explains. "There is also a moist canned food diet, which is fairly expensive. If you feed a combination of two (pelleted, powdered, moist) with some leafy greens as a supplement, you'll be doing fine."

Bowker cautions people who believe they must give their animals additional calcium supplements. "Too much calcium will deplete the phosphorus level in the animal and that can be a problem," he says. "If you're feeding a balanced diet and the animal is eating the correct variety, very little extra calcium, if any, will be needed."

Feeding your iguana properly takes knowledge, thought, and planning. Unless you use the new commercial diets, it also takes some work. But doing it right is worth the trouble in the end. You will have a healthy, happy animal, not one that is slowly losing the battle to stay healthy because it isn't being fed correctly.

CAN MY IGUANA BE TRAINED?

An iguana is not going to act like the family dog. It is not going to come on command, sit, stay, roll over, and do some of the other things dogs will do. However, if handled properly, most iguanas can become friendly pets that bond to their owners. With persistence, some can be conditioned to give the response you want from them.

It all begins with handling. If you don't handle your iguana from the time you first get it, the animal will be nervous and shy away from your hand. It may even become nasty as it gets older. Larry Wieder, who has bred and raised a variety of animals, has been giving a home to unwanted iguanas for several years. He has not only observed their behavior and worked with them firsthand, but has also seen some of the mistakes their original owners have made.

"People should handle the iguana as much as they can," Wieder says. "The animal needs that bonding to be friendly. I've taken in some nasty ones that were almost never handled. But if you begin working with them they get used to you and don't object to being petted and handled. I know a man who gives his iguana the run of the house. The animal comes up to him, just like a dog, and will sit with him when he's watching television. So they can be a very good pet with the right owner."

A few other training methods can be used to condition your iguana. Some people have learned to move their iguana with a target stick. This is a stick with a ball attached to the top. If you have a male iguana who is being nasty during breeding season, or an iguana you are nervous about handling, you might try this method. Some iguanas will simply follow the target stick if it is moved along the ground in front of them. People will use it to get their iguana into a carrier for a trip to the vet, or even back into its enclosure if it has been let out. It doesn't work for everyone, but it's worth a try.

There are also ways to reinforce behaviors that you want your iguana to repeat. Some people have had success with a method they call "clicker training." Dog trainers will often use this same method. You need a little plastic box that makes a sharp, clicking sound. Iguanas do not seem to object to the sound, especially once they begin to associate it with a food treat. You can also use another sound source, even making a clicking sound with your tongue. But it must be a single, sharp sound.

You might withhold one of your iguana's favorite foods from its regular meal, such as greens, and use that as a treat. When your iguana does something you want repeated, quickly make the clicking sound and follow it immediately with a treat. Soon, the animal will associate the click with a treat and respond accordingly.

Maybe you won't get your iguana to roll over using this method, but you can train it to do things such as coming toward you, climbing on your arm, or walking into a carrier. Don't expect too much at first. Your iguana will not learn as quickly as a dog. But if you keep working with it you will have a better pet, for several reasons. The training sessions will give you more of a bond with your animal. At the same time, you'll enjoy your iguana more and teach it to do some simple behaviors on command. It's worth the effort.

WHAT IF I CAN'T KEEP MY
IGUANA ANYMORE?

In most areas of the United States iguanas cannot survive on their own in the wild. If you decide you can no longer properly care for your iguana, don't let it loose. If you do that, chances are it won't live very long.

"The biggest problem with iguanas is that many pet store workers won't tell a customer that the animal will grow to 5 or 6 feet," Larry Wieder says. "They look cute at 5 or 6 inches, but as soon as they outgrow the small aquarium many are put in, the problems start. Too many people still mistakenly feel they can live in a 10- or 20-gallon aquarium their entire lives."

Other problems are simply people or kids becoming tired of them as pets, or males becoming nasty during the breeding cycle. Many are not cared for properly at this point, and by the time the owner starts looking for a way out, the animal is already sick.

"I actually found one on the side of the road one time," Wieder says. "Unfortunately, it was already too sick to save it. Some that can be saved have scars on their back from heat lamps being placed too close or show physical deformities from the wrong kind of diet."

People who no longer want their iguana should take time to find it a good home. There are rescue centers in some cities or perhaps a local veterinarian who will find a proper home. Zoos usually do not want them. They probably have enough. If your animal is lucky, there will be someone like Larry Wieder around. He now has 14 discarded iguanas who are getting the proper care and proper diet so they can live out their lives.

"Education is the key," Wieder says. "Before anyone buys an iguana, they should know exactly what they are getting and the kind of care the animal will need to remain happy and healthy."

Unfortunately, not everyone does this.

SNAKES

Snake is the common name for any reptile belonging to the suborder Serpentes. All snakes have long cylindrical bodies and no external limbs. Most snakes move along the ground using an undulating crawl, called the serpentine method. To move this way, the snake pushes against the ground on the back side of each curve or undulation, and flows smoothly forward. The fastest snake can only move at about 8 miles (13 km) per hour. Most humans can run faster than that. This slithering effect, however, is one reason that people fear snakes.

The skeleton of the snake is also different from that of other animals. There are a large number of vertebrae, never fewer than 100 and sometimes more than 430. Except for the first two, each vertebra has a pair of ribs. The skeleton is light in structure and modified to give the animal great freedom of movement.

There are many different kinds of snakes, from the harmless garter snake to the huge boa constrictors and anacondas. There are land and water snakes, poisonous and nonpoisonous species. Different types of snakes can be found in nearly every corner of the world. Only some of them, however, make acceptable pets.

"Snakes require less care than any other animal," says reptile expert Bob Bowker. "They don't have to be fed daily, just require a heat source and clean water. In fact, some have to be fed just once a week or even once every two weeks. Many respond to gentle handling and become very calm."

Most snakes have very good vision and an acute sense of smell. They smell by flicking the tongue out, picking up odors, then carrying them to the roof of the mouth. There, the tongue contacts a sensory receptor called Jacobson's organ. Snakes are deaf to airborne sounds, but can pick up vibrations through the ground or whatever they are resting upon. Some vipers, boas, and pythons have another sense organ. It is a heat receptor that

can perceive small differences in temperature. That helps them locate warm-blooded prey at night.

Snakes are carnivorous. They eat a variety of animal life, anything from insects and spiders, to snails and frogs, to mice and rats. Because of a special, hinged jaw, snakes can swallow animals whole that are actually larger than their heads and bodies.

PICKING A PET SNAKE

Some snakes are off limits as a pet for the average family. Rare and endangered snakes are protected by law and shouldn't be in a private home. If someone tries to sell you a snake you are not sure about, it is easy to find a list of endangered animals to check it out. In addition, no amateur hobbyist or first-time owner should buy a poisonous snake. A poisonous snake can be a danger to you, your family, and your friends.

There are, however, a wide variety from which to choose. The most common snakes kept by hobbyists are the members of the constrictor family, including boas, pythons, and rat and milk snakes. Other popular snakes kept as pets are the racer, gopher, and garter varieties. However, the boa constrictor and pythons reach very large sizes in captivity and take up a great deal of space. It is suggested that someone keeping a huge snake should have at least five years of experience with other types of small, harmless snakes.

Milk snakes, king snakes, and corn snakes are also possibilities as a first pet snake. The smaller ball python is said to have the most predictable and even temperament of all the python species. As a result, certain species of snakes almost always retain a gentle, calm, laid-back nature when raised from infancy in captivity. It is extremely important to get some solid opinions from real experts before choosing a first snake as a pet.

You should look for a few other things when selecting a snake as a pet. Try to be sure that the snake you pick is eating regularly and without problems. This won't be easy because snakes do not eat every day. So if you are buying from a pet shop you might not get a demonstration. It's not like giving a dog a treat. Maybe the person at the pet shop will help you select a suitable pet.

Always try to pick a snake that appears healthy and hardy. If a snake, or any reptile, appears ill, chances are that you won't be able to bring it back to full health. Poor or incorrect treatment in captivity might cause health problems that won't go away. Only a veterinarian or reptile expert should work with an unhealthy animal.

In addition, always make sure you know exactly what kind of snake you are getting. Before making a final decision, learn all you can about that species. That way, you will know something about its temperament, how big it will get, what it eats, and what kind of pet it will make.

Generally speaking, snakes do not need a great deal of room as they are not high-activity animals. The enclosure should be large enough to include certain necessary items and for the snake to stretch out and move about somewhat. Glass aquariums make very good enclosures for snakes because you can easily see the animal and also maintain the correct temperature and humidity.

"In short, a snake's needs are similar to other reptiles," Bob Bowker explains. "They need a basking site, a cool-down section, and a large vessel of water, big enough to hold their entire body."

As with iguana enclosures, a piece of indoor-outdoor carpeting or Astroturf makes the best base. You can also use paper towels, terry-cloth towels, or even butcher paper. All these items can be easily cleaned or changed. Never use a substrate such as kitty litter, wood shavings, or crushed corncobs. These items can trap moisture and dirt, thus becoming breeding grounds for external parasites. They also can be inadvertently eaten while the snake is feeding on its own food.

With snakes, you can use a hot rock as a heat source. They will do better with it than an iguana, for which it doesn't work. But you still have to be sure it won't get too hot and burn your pet. You can also put a heating pad under the aquarium with a towel in between. Tropical snakes (boas, pythons) should be kept at a daytime temperature between 80 and 85 degrees F (27 and 30°C) with a high humidity, with a nighttime temperature between 70 and 75 degrees F (21 and 24°C). American snakes

will do well if their environment is maintained between 70 and 80 degrees.

Larger enclosures will need heat lamps or other types of heaters. As with other reptiles, snakes must be kept at the correct temperature to keep their activity level high and to help them digest their food. So the proper temperature is crucial.

Light is important, as well. The best light for a snake is the natural light of the sun. If this isn't available, then you should use an artificial, ultraviolet light source. You can usually buy this type of light at a good pet shop. Once again, you should try to simulate the snake's natural environment, which means 10–12 hours of light and 12–14 hours of darkness each day.

MAKING THE ENVIRONMENT MORE NATURAL

Besides a heat and light source, the liner of the enclosure, and water, you can also add some additional materials to make your pet feel at home. Many snakes enjoy climbing on branches, which can be cut from hardwood trees or made from artificial materials. They also enjoy grapevine, hanging ropes, and shelves built along the sides of the enclosure. These additions will give your pet snake a more natural environment and make it much more fun for you to watch as it explores its home.

Some young snakes also like their privacy. A hiding place, such as a hollowed-out log or a box, will give the animal a chance to get away from it all.

Another way to house your pet snake is to make a home terrarium. A terrarium is a container in which living plants and creatures are kept in an environment as nearly like their natural habitat as possible. There are many ways to make a terrarium.

You can use a glass aquarium as long as it has a secure mesh top for ventilation. Some people prefer to use wood or another material on three sides, with glass in front. One thing that should never be used is wire. Snakes can injure themselves trying to push through the openings in the wire.

If you decide to make your terrarium all natural, you should find someone who has already done it successfully. You can visit a nearby zoo, where snakes are exhibited in their natural environment. Or seek out the advice of a naturalist who has worked with snakes. An expert can tell you how to set up your terrarium, what kinds of plants to include, and how to maintain it properly.

Setting up a natural home for your pet snake can be challenging and fun. If you do it correctly, it will make your pet happier and allow you to enjoy having it even more.

HOW DO I FEED MY SNAKE?

Feeding captive snakes is not nearly as complex as feeding iguanas. In the wild, snakes eat live prey, capturing and swallowing it whole. However, putting live prey in your snake's enclosure may cause problems. For one thing, you may not feel comfortable doing it. You may not want to take a live animal and feed it to another animal. Even though this is what happens in the wild, it is not quite the same in your home.

In addition, if you put a live rodent in your snake's enclosure and the snake is not ready to eat, the rodent can inflict some serious bites on the snake's head, causing injuries that could need medical attention. According to Bob Bowker, there is yet another reason not to use live animals as food for pet snakes.

"To introduce live animals can sometimes sharpen the snake's feeding response," Bowker explains. "That will make the animal more prone to biting and might make your handling of your pet a little more risky."

Bowker, like many other experts, recommends purchasing prefrozen prey for your snake. "Thaw the frozen rodent under hot tap water," Bowker suggests. "Then pat it dry with a paper towel and feed it to your snake while it's still warm. Sometimes you might have to move it with a pair of tongs until the snake notices and then takes it."

Once you have your snake eating its food, you might only have to feed it once a week or once every two weeks. If you don't handle your snake regularly, then you should take more care when feeding. A hungry snake that anticipates food might strike at your hand as soon as the enclosure is opened. If you handle your snake regularly, you probably won't have this problem.

On the whole, captive snakes will remain healthy if they eat the food you offer. They are not nearly as prone to nutritional problems as are many other reptiles. This is because they are feeding on whole prey, the same as they would in the wild. That is what makes feeding a pet snake relatively easy.

WHY DOES MY SNAKE SHED ITS SKIN?

Don't be alarmed if one day you go in to look at your snake and it seems to be growing right out of its skin. The periodic shedding of the outer portion of their skin is something snakes do regularly. It's an activity that is controlled by hormones and is associated with the growth of the snake. Most snakes shed their skin four to eight times a year. Young snakes shed more often than older ones simply because they are growing faster in the first few years of their lives.

For a healthy snake, shedding is not difficult. The skin will usually come off in one piece. A snake with injuries to the skin or one being kept at the wrong temperature and humidity levels may have some difficulty. So will snakes that are ill or under a great deal of stress. In these cases, the skin comes off in pieces, and some can remain attached to the underlying skin and eyes.

Before shedding, a snake is usually inactive for a week or two. The eyes will have a dull, bluish white appearance, and the skin on the whole appears dull. The snake will rub against rough objects or surfaces in its enclosure to help shed the skin. Shedding begins at the head, followed by the rest of the body. It is just another natural act that occurs in the wild. In captivity, you can have the joy of watching your pet snake shed its skin as part of the growing process.

Snakes are not difficult pets to keep if you learn about them and give them a healthy environment. The right kind of snake will respond well to handling and will give you hours of enjoyment by observing its daily activities. As with all reptiles, snakes should be kept only by people who are and will remain dedicated to their welfare. The responsibility never ends. You should never forget that any confined animal relies totally on its keeper for its well-being.

TURTLES

Turtle and tortoise are the names given to reptiles that have a hard shell enclosing their internal organs. Like other reptiles, they are ancient animals whose ancestors go back some 200 million years. Scientists believe that turtles existed even before the great dinosaurs walked the earth. Through it all, turtles have continued to adapt to changing conditions in the world and have flourished. So this is a tough animal and one that has been kept as a pet for many years.

There are many different kinds of turtles. Some are land turtles, while others, called aquatic turtles, live mainly in the water. The size of turtles can also vary greatly. The common box turtle of North America is only about 6 inches (15 cm) in length, sometimes even smaller. Yet the giant sea-dwelling leatherneck can grow to a length of 8 feet (2.4 meters).

PHYSICAL CHARACTERISTICS

The upper shell of the turtle is called the *carapace*. In most cases, the head, limbs, and tail of the animal can be completely withdrawn into the carapace for protection. The lower shell, which is flat or a bit concave, is called the *plastron*. The two parts of the shell are connected to the vertebrae and ribs. The shell has two layers. The inner layer is bony, and the sections of it contain the animal's dermal bones. Then there is an overlapping, outer layer, made up of a hornlike material that shields the turtle from its enemies.

Turtles have no teeth. They use their jaws to chew. Even the snapping turtle, which can give a bad bite, doesn't have teeth. Instead, it has very large, sharp jaws. Unlike snakes, turtles can hear, but they have poor eyesight. They are fairly intelligent animals with a long life span. Box turtles can live up to 100 years, while red-eared sliders usually live about 20. To have a turtle as

a pet means you are making a long commitment to that animal.

A water turtle can be identified by its webbed feet (for swimming), while a land turtle has separate toes. The difference in keeping the two types of turtles as pets is that land turtles must live in a terrarium, while aquatic turtles must be housed in an aquarium. According to reptile expert Bob Bowker, water turtles are a great deal of fun to watch.

"They're animated and responsive, often sticking their heads out of the water and looking at you," Bowker says.

Of all the reptiles, turtles present the greatest risk of salmonella infection. One reason is that turtles in pet shops are often under stress, increasing the chance of bacterial infection. In addition, turtles tend to drop their feces in water, which can become contaminated quickly. This can be another source of infection if the water is not changed immediately. All of the rules for protection against salmonella given earlier apply also to pet turtles.

PICKING OUT A PET TURTLE

Years ago, people would buy baby turtles and place them in a small plastic bowl. It had water surrounding a plastic ramp where the turtle could climb up to dry off. Sometimes they would put them in a bowl with a rock or two sitting in the water. It seemed easy to just throw in some food and care for them. Unfortunately, nothing could be farther from the truth. Most of those turtles didn't live very long.

Before you pick out a pet turtle, you should know the amount of time it will take to properly house, feed, and care for it. Some experts maintain that turtles are not the right pets for young children. However, both child and parents must work together to understand and care for the animal. If the turtle is intended to be the child's pet, the parents must also know about the care of the animal and check it regularly to make sure it is being cared for properly. In many cases, parents and child can learn together.

You cannot go out and buy a turtle any time you want. Some turtles native to cold winter climates hibernate, much the way bears do. That means they spend the winter in a dormant state. Experts advise against buying a turtle in the fall, winter, or early spring. That is when the turtle would be hibernating in its natural state. If you see turtles in pet shops during these months, they are very likely to be stressed. In addition, they could be suffering from dehydration and starvation at this time. It's better to buy a pet-shop turtle during the late spring and summer. Chances are the animals will be healthier then.

When you buy from a pet shop, pick the turtle up. It should feel solid, not like a lightweight empty shell. Tug gently on a back leg. The turtle should pull the leg away strongly. Look for any swellings on the face or limbs. There should not be any. The eyes should be open and clear, and appear alert. There should be no cuts or splits or cracks in the shell.

If you insist on buying a turtle during the hibernating months, go to a captive breeder or owner who has a reputation for selling healthy animals.

IS IT DIFFICULT TO HOUSE AND FEED MY TURTLE?

Many species of turtles are kept in captivity. It's impossible to discuss all of them here. For the purposes of this book, two turtles will be considered. Both are native to the United States.

They are the box turtle and the semiaquatic red-eared slider. These are two of the most popular turtles kept as pets.

The American box turtle is found throughout the eastern, central, and southwestern United States, as well as the northern parts of Mexico. It is not entirely a land turtle in that, in the wild, it needs access to a body of water. It also prefers woody grasslands with dry, sandy soil on top with humid earth below. The box turtle is an outdoor animal that needs sunlight for health and well-being. To simply house it in a glass aquarium is not a good idea.

For one thing, you cannot enjoy the turtle's inquisitive personality if it is kept in a tank. It will most likely go into a corner and try to scratch its way out. Finally, it will give up and become more like a rock than a turtle, just sitting still. Under stress in this environment, many stop eating and soon fall victim to stress-related illnesses.

Most forest-dwelling box turtles live in warm, moist, and shady environments for a good part of the year. In the wild, a box turtle has a home range and knows the location of every rock, tree, and watering hole. Their water source tends to be a permanent pond or stream. The turtles eat foods that are found in the woods and near the streams. Among their natural foods are grubs, worms, fallen fruits, berries, and mushrooms.

If you take the time, you can create a mini-version of the turtle's natural environment outdoors. The enclosure should be on the east or south side of the building. Like the iguana, turtles need exposure to natural sunlight to help metabolize vitamin D_3, which is used for calcium uptake. There should also be partial shade so that the turtle is not forced to stay out in the sun all day long.

The enclosure should be as large as you and your parents can afford to make it. The walls should be high enough so the turtle cannot stretch up to the top and pull itself over the rim. The sides can be made of wooden boards, plastic siding, bricks, or cement. Do not use lattice or wire as the turtle can injure itself trying to squeeze through the holes. The area around the perimeter of the enclosure should be lined with recessed paving tiles or bricks. That way, when the turtle digs at the wall, it will soon know it cannot escape.

The enclosure must contain water and feeding stations. The water station can be a shallow flowerpot saucer recessed slightly into the ground. The feeding station can simply be a gravel area where a shallow plate of food can be placed. Shrubs and some vegetables can be grown in the partially shaded area. There should also be a hide box for each turtle and some sturdy logs for climbing or digging under. And don't forget some kind of wire top that will keep other animals and small children out of the enclosure.

The red-eared slider needs both a warm, dry area and a large pool of water. In the wild, it will go to water that the sun warms quickly every day. In captivity, you will have to provide a warm enclosure and warm place for the turtle to dry off after it has been in the water. Sliders can be kept in an aquarium, at least a

20-gallon (76-liter) size at the beginning. There should be a wet end (the pool) and a dry end. You can use clean aquarium rock and gravel to build the slope from the wet end to the dry.

The resting platform should be smooth. Rough rocks can scratch the turtle's shell and allow bacteria to form and fungal infections to begin. Water must be as deep as your turtle is long. If the top shell of the slider is 6 inches (15 cm) long, the pool must be at least 6 inches deep so that your turtle can swim around freely. Then, as the turtle grows, you will have to increase its water area. Eventually, this will mean getting a larger aquarium.

A number of other things are required to keep a red-eared slider. The water must be filtered and changed frequently. Commercial filters are available at most pet shops. If you filter well and feed your turtle in another tank, you might be able to siphon out 25–50 percent of the water each week. Then you must empty and clean the entire tank every third or fourth week. If you feed in the live-in tank, you still must filter, but should change the water completely once a week.

Water temperature must be maintained between 75 and 86 degrees F (24 and 30°C). You'll need a good heater and a thermometer to make sure this is done correctly. If the water is too cold, the slider won't eat. If it's too warm, it can hurt the animal. The turtle's room must be kept above 75 degrees or, if not, the tank area must be kept that warm. There should also be a basking light that will allow the temperature to reach between 85 and 88 degrees F (30 and 31°C). Constant low temperatures (between 65 and 72 degrees F, or 18 and 22°C) can cause turtles to stop eating and develop respiratory infections.

Sliders can also be put outside in the sun when the temperatures are warm. You can move the entire tank outside, or transfer the turtle to an outside tub with both basking and swimming areas. If you can't do this, you should consider a full-spectrum fluorescent light for the correct metabolism of calcium.

FEEDING TIME

As with other captive animals, turtles should be fed a balanced diet. But they should not be overfed. A number of commercial feeds on the market provide a good staple for turtles. If you have a box turtle in a natural, outdoor habitat, it can forage for grubs and worms, and you can plant vegetable matter such as collard greens, parsley, strawberry plants, clover, and alfalfa. Or you can grow these things in a garden and feed them to your turtle.

Red-eared sliders and other aquatic turtles can also eat commercial foods. One type, a floating food that comes in pellets, sticks, or tablets, is specially formulated for turtles and doesn't decompose in water as fast as some other foods. Other types of floating food sticks are available as well. Water turtles can also be fed live feeder fish, such as guppies or goldfish. Protein can also be supplied by finely chopped raw lean beef and cooked chicken. Never feed raw chicken, which may carry salmonella.

Greens such as collard, mustard, and dandelion, as well as shredded carrots, squash, and green beans are also excellent. Vitamin supplements can be added twice a week. Very young turtles may be fed daily. Most turtles, however, should not be fed every day. An overweight turtle is an unhealthy one. Every two or three days (depending on the turtle's activity level) is just fine.

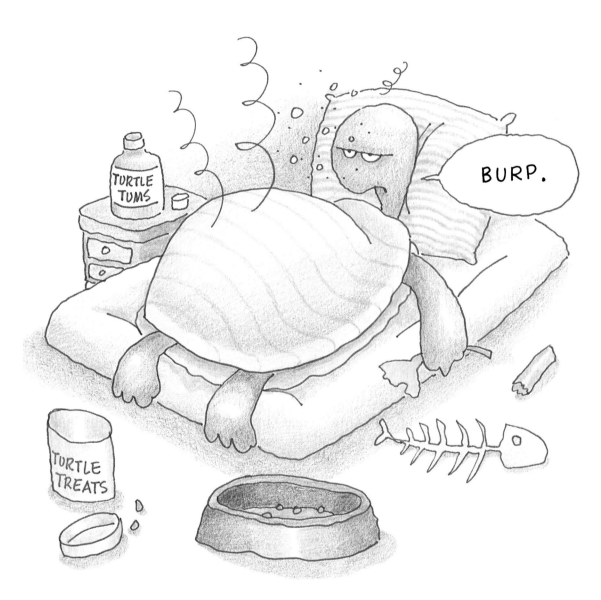

When picking up your turtle, always support its body with both hands. Don't just hold it in the middle of its lower shell. Some people think the turtles are going through swimming motions when they flail their legs in the air. But they are actually looking for something solid to stand on and become quite stressed when they can't find it. As with other animals, the more you handle your turtle and speak to it, the more it will come to know you.

If you think that something is wrong with your turtle, try to find a veterinarian who works with them regularly. You can get a referral from a zoo or maybe another veterinarian. Or you can contact the Association of Reptile and Amphibian Veterinarians

to find one near you. At any rate, don't try to play doctor. If your animal is sick or injured, it needs professional help.

Turtles that hibernate in their natural habitat (where the winters are cold) will want to hibernate even in captivity. These turtles will be in a state of hibernation from late fall to early spring. In the wild, box turtles seek a sheltered place, like a gopher hole, or a hollowed-out log in which to hide and hibernate. Red-eared sliders will dig down into the mud to hibernate in the wild.

If you notice your box turtle becoming more motionless and passive in the fall, it may be getting ready to hibernate. It will also begin eating less. To make sure, some experts suggest bathing the turtle in 75–79 degree F (24–26°C) water 10 minutes at a time for four straight days. Then turn off heating and lights and leave it for three days. After three days, if the turtle becomes more passive and motionless and is hardly eating, it is time for hibernation.

By this time, your turtle should be indoors, in a cool area such as a basement with the temperature between 50 and 55 degrees F (10 and 13°C). It should be in a high box with clean water, but no food. Remember, turtles cannot digest food properly at this low temperature. The area should be dark and left that way until the end of March.

"Some people who don't have the facilities to hibernate the turtle will keep it going all winter," Bob Bowker explains. "You have to simulate an outdoor summer environment inside your

home, with the correct heat and light, and a natural area in which your turtle can live. If you can do it, however, hibernation is the more natural state."

To test to see if your slider is ready, turn off the lights and heat in the aquarium. Wait until the water reaches room temperature. Then set the temperature below 64 degrees F (18°C) for a few days. If the turtle is passive and motionless, and hardly eating, it is ready to hibernate.

"You must have a hibernation aquarium with about 5 or 6 inches of mud or silt from a pond," says Bob Bowker. "The turtle will bury itself in the mud. The temperature should be kept between 50 and 60 degrees during hibernation. Just make sure the water stays clean. From my experience, however, most people with sliders just keep them going as usual throughout the winter. They seem to survive it nicely."

Hibernation of some species is just another aspect of turtle-keeping that is not easy. Turtles are long-lived animals, so if you obtain one and accept the responsibility of ownership, you will have the animal for a long time. As with other reptiles, the entire family should know about the turtle and share the responsibility for its care.

Reptiles are not throwaway pets. You don't get an iguana, snake, or turtle on a whim, tire of it, and forget about it. The worst thing you can do with a reptile is not give it the proper care. Then, you are sentencing the animal to illness and a slow death. The fact that they have survived for millions of years in the wild is a tribute to their toughness. In captivity, however, they depend on you. They are interesting creatures to keep, to watch, and to enjoy. You will learn a great deal by observing them.

However, if you decide you can no longer keep your reptile, don't just release it. The animal will die. Try to contact a herpetological club or rescue society dedicated to finding homes for reptiles and amphibians. If you no longer want your animals, finding it a good home would be the final act of love you could give it.

FIND OUT MORE

WEB SITES

Reptiles, Among Other Things www.reptilecare.com

Reptile Rescue www.reptilerescue.on.ca

Iguana Information Hotline
www.geocities.com/RainForest/9008/hotline.com

Reptile Rapsody, Reptile Rescue http://reptile1.webjump.com

BOOKS

Green Iguana: The Ultimate Owners Manual. James W. Hatfield.
    Portland, OR: Dunthorpe Press, 1997.
Iguanas: Everything About Selection, Care, Nutrition, Diseases, Breeding &
    Behavior. Richard D. Bartlett. Happague, NY: Barron's
    Educational Series, Inc, 1998.
Snake. Christopher Mattison. New York: D.K. Publishing, Inc,
    1999.

Snakes: Everything About Selection, Care, Nutrition, Diseases, Breeding &
   Behavior. Richard D. Bartlett, Patricia P. Bartlett.
   Happague, NY: Barron's Educational Series, Inc, 1998.
Turtles and Tortoises: Everything About Selection, Care, Nutrition, Breeding
   & Behavior. Richard D. Bartlett, Patricia P. Bartlett.
   Happague, NY: Barron's Educational Series, Inc, 1996.
Turtles: How to Take Care of Them and Understand Them. Hartmut
   Wilke, Matthew M. Vriends. Happague, NY: Barron's
   Educational Series, Inc, 1991.

INDEX